GRAMMAR—

THE WRITE

CONNECTION

MARTHA C. DARTER

Grammar – The Write Connection

Martha C. Darter

Copyright © 2011, Martha C. Darter
ISBN 978-1-257-62718-9

Dedication

To my daughter who said, "I can't teach English from this textbook; the kids just aren't getting it. Write something I can USE." To Susan, who gave invaluable advice and guidance. To the rest of my family, for their support and encouragement.

Acknowledgments

Some of the worksheets are adapted from material written by Patrick McManus, Jean Sheppard, and Peter Hathaway Capstick. (My apologies for tweaking your text.) Your humor helped relieve the unutterable boredom of typical English assignments.

My gratitude goes to Koreena Stowell, who helped solve numerous issues involving my limited computer skills and the vagaries of my somewhat elderly PC.

A special thank you goes to Miriam Foster, long-time friend and colleague, for her enthusiastic support and promotion of this approach to English teaching. Thanks also goes to friends and colleagues Kathy Kahn, Deanne Hawks, and Marj Welch, who bought into the program and used it in their classes. And, to my students, many thanks for helping me learn to teach English.

Preface

First of all, no such thing as a "good" English textbook exists. Only a few of the universally poor quality offerings can be adequately used, and often a teacher does not get to choose which of the overall deplorable books is the least offensive!

English grammar is and always has been English grammar. Period. There's no re-inventing the wheel here. English grammar just IS. Sure, the terminology might have changed, the emphasis has changed, and the format has certainly changed. But, it's the same old same old, déjà vu all over again!

English grammar is generally not taught at the college level. In fact, you'd be hard-pressed to <u>find</u> a college-level course dealing with it. (I found a Transformational Grammar class once; I loved it!) Instead, the prospective teacher takes a multitude of literature courses, most of which involve material that is not really suitable for English teaching, grades 7 through 12. A couple of composition classes are required, and few other writing classes may be available. Of course, many "papers" are required in those lit courses, yet any classes concerning how to teach writing -- let alone how to teach language -- are conspicuously absent. Unless a teacher has been fortunate enough to encounter an "old-school" grammarian and/or a no-nonsense writing instructor in his 7-12th grade school years, he probably really doesn't know how to write very well himself, let alone how to tell an adverb from an aardvark!

Why the emphasis on grammar? Isn't that old-fashioned, passé, unnecessary? "Can't we just 'spill our guts' on paper, penning touchy-feely stuff and not worry about mechanics? Won't the reader know what I mean?" Wrong. Grammar will not simply "go away." For one thing, huge emphasis is currently placed on the No Child Left Behind concept, on teacher accountability, and on standardized testing results. The ISAT comes to mind -- and yes, they still ask grammar questions, lots of them. Most importantly, knowing grammar is essential for a teacher to improve a student's writing. If a student doesn't know what an introductory subordinate clause is, how can an instructor teach him to follow it with a comma? (Note this sentence example.) If a student isn't able to recognize a complete sentence, how can he avoid run-ons or fragments? If a student doesn't know what a transition is, how can he learn the nuances of the paragraph hook or the idea hook to make his writing more sophisticated or confront the perils of parallel structure. If these examples leave you wondering what the heck I'm talking about, you were probably understandably frightened by an English textbook at an early age!

What's a teacher to do? First of all, put the English book on the shelf to use for "reference." You may be able to utilize some of the usage, composition, and spelling material. Then start at the beginning, at the ground floor, at the start of grammar --Parts of Speech. (Observe the correct use of parallel structure in that sentence!)

Quite a number of exercises are included for the punctuation section and a few for the other grammar sections. Feel free to add more of your own. Most of the exercises in texts contain material that is usually boring, sometimes contradictory, and mostly irrelevant as well as sometimes inaccurate. They are sentences not of the real world, sentences that no one you know would really write contrivances of a pedantic professor.

What to do? For years, I generated my own exercises at the 11th and 12th grade levels, trying to write sentences that were interesting, entertaining, humorous, and/or provocative. Then my daughter, a very successful 7th/8th grade English teacher, provided an answer: Student-generated material! They love it! And, they will really <u>learn</u> it if they have to come up with their own group's sentences, give them to the other students, and grade them. You've got "ownership," "collaborative learning," lots of "guided practice," and no sheaves of papers to grade at home when you'd rather watch CSI.

Disclaimer: I don't' have a Master's Degree in English. I do have thirty-plus years of teaching experience in English in public schools at the 11th and 12th grade levels. I have taught regular English classes, Applied English classes, Remedial English classes, Honors English classes, and all kinds of literature classes. I have received Teacher of the Year Awards, Student/Teacher Recognition Awards, a nomination for Idaho Teacher of the Year, Student-Teacher Preparation Awards, and Inspirational Teacher Awards. So, big deal, right? Mainly, I have loved working with my students and helping them achieve success in their college-level composition classes (or "exam out" of them) and in the language demands of their workplace. I learned English by teaching it to my students (although I did have a couple of fine old-school grammar teachers in my background), and I learned to teach writing that way too.

SEQUENCE FOR TEACHING ENGLISH

I. Parts of Speech
    A. Nouns
    B. Verbs
    C. Adverbs
    D. Adjectives
    E. Prepositions (and prepositional phrases)
    F. Conjunctions
    G. Interjections
    H. Pronouns

II. Sentences
    A. Complete/Incomplete
    B. Subject/Predicates
    C. Parts of Sentences/Sentence Patterns
        1. Subject
        2. Verb
        3. Predicate Nouns/Predicate Adjectives
        4. Direct Objects
        5. Indirect Objects
        6. *Object Complements

III. Phrases, Clusters, and Clauses
    A. Prepositional Phrases (revisited)
    B. Verbals and Verbal Phrases
        1. Participles
        2. Gerunds
        3. Infinitives
    C. Noun Clusters (Appositives)
    D. Verb Clusters (Participial Phrases)
    E. Adjective Phrases
    F. Clauses
        1. Independent

        2. Dependent
           a. Subordinate -- adverb
           b. Relative -- adjective

IV. Structure of Sentences

    A. Simple
    B. Compound
    C. Complex
    D. Compound-Complex

V. Diagramming for Fun! Hey! Some people do Crosswords!

VI. Punctuation

    A. Basic Rules
    B. Other Marks and Squiggles

VII. Mechanics

    A. Capitalization
    B. Some Notes on Spelling
    C. Glossary (or do with usage)

VIII. Usage

    A. Agreement
    B. Pronouns
    C. Verbs
    D. Modifiers

IX. Step-Up to Writing!

    A. Transitions
    B. The Process

Other Marks and Squiggles

This information is found in most English texts or handbooks: apostrophes, parentheses, brackets, colons, underlining, dashes, question marks, exclamation points, and single/double quotation marks.
•

Mechanics and Usage

Get those old textbooks off the shelf for these:
    Capitalization
    Agreement
    Pronoun Usage
    Verb Usage
    Usage Glossary – includes words often confused or misused, etc.

WRITING

STEP-UP to Writing is an excellent program to help students organize their writing, most useful for grades 7-9 and even beyond. For high school sophomores and juniors, check out Lucille Vaughan Payne's <u>The Lively Art of Writing</u> series. For college-bound seniors, get Payne's <u>The Lively Art of Writing – Effecting Style</u> and use it as your bible for first semester. It is absolutely superb!

    The material in this book has been successfully used for students 8 through 12. It is presented in its basic form although additional exercises for various levels of student abilities should certainly be included. Adaptations for more advanced students involve, for example, more difficult practice, an in-depth study of verbals, and more combination punctuation rule practice. On the other hand, younger students may benefit from simpler assignments. Some suggested assignments have been included. It seems that this information bears much repetition as many students wake up to a brand-new world every school year.

PARTS OF SPEECH

All you <u>ever</u> (<u>never</u> ? ☺) wanted to know about …

NOUNS:

Definition: A word that names a person, place, thing, or idea.

Test: Is there such a thing as (a, an) _____?
 Is there such a thing as a *rock*? Is there such a thing as an *eagle*? Is there such a thing as *hope*?

Derivational (!) Suffixes:
 -ment: government _____
 -tion: realization _____
 -er/or: writer/doctor _____
 -ity: unity _____
 -ence: difference _____
 -ance: romance _____
 -ness: happiness _____
 -ist: dentist _____
 -ism: Buddhism _____

Lexical Suffixes: -s or -es / -ies for plurals, -'s or s' for possessives. You can learn about plurals and possessives now or in Mechanics, depending on your teacher!

Use in a sentence:
 Subject
 Predicate Noun (Nominative)
 Direct Object
 Indirect Object
 Object of the Preposition

Position in a sentence:
 In front of the verb

After a verb
After a preposition

Types:
- Proper and Common Nouns:

    Proper Noun: names a particular person, place, thing, or idea and *starts with a capital letter.*

    Ex: Ollie Hopnoodle, Pontoon Saloon, Jump-off Bridge

    Common Noun: names a general person, place, thing, or idea and does *not* start with a capital letter.

    Ex: boy, boat, bridge

- Concrete and Abstract Nouns:

    Concrete Noun: can be seen, weighed, measured, smelled, tasted, or touched.

    Ex; photograph, house, rose, banana, horse

    Abstract Noun: names an idea, feeling, quality or characteristic:

    Ex: love, fun, freedom, beauty, hope, truth

- Collective Noun: names a group

    Ex: team, family, flock

- Compound Noun*:

    Compound Noun: made up of more than one word.

    Ex: grandmother, football, stepfather, Greenland, self-control, Chief Joseph

*NOTE: Currently, there is some controversy concerning whether or not a compound noun made up of two separate words is a compound noun or just an adjective and a noun.

Ex: fire drill, chain reaction--probably compound nouns since both words are generally used as nouns.

Ex: electric drill, sudden reaction--probably not compound, just an adjective and a noun.

Ex: potty chair--who knows? Potty can be a verb (I pottied at 6:00.) or a noun (Do you have to go to the potty?), but here it seems to be used as an adjective. Bet they won't put that one on the ISAT anyhow! ☺

What should you do? Follow your teacher's advice and your own best judgment. It probably doesn't matter that much in the whole scheme of things anyway!

KEEP IN MIND: A NOUN CAN BE BOTH ... common and abstract/ proper and concrete/ collective and concrete, etc

Noun Practice   Name _____

Use this worksheet for Noun practice. Follow your teacher's directions. For example, you could underline all Concrete Nouns and circle Abstract Nouns, double underlining Proper Nouns. Have fun!

1. Humpy Hogroll was the only kid at Gilbert Grunge Grammar School who tipped the scales at two hundred pounds in the fourth grade.

2. The kids didn't tease him much though; he would just back them up against a wall and lean on them until their eyes bugged out and they couldn't breathe.

3. That happened to Ollie Hopnoggin once, and every time Humpy would get close to him, he got that deer-in-the-headlight look.

4. Ollie was in love with Mimi Stinkmouse, and she thought he was pretty cute too--although he didn't weigh sixty-five pounds soaking wet.

5. Unfortunately, Humpy was pretty crazy about Mimi himself and kept a close watch on Ollie.

6. If he thought Ollie was a getting a bit too friendly with Mimi, he sort of cut him out of the herd of fourth graders and nudged him toward the blackboard.

7. Ollie learned to dodge and depart in a hurry; in fact, he learned most of his football skills in the fourth grade and was the best running back on the high school team years later.

8. Humpy was on the team too as he had developed his leaning technique into pretty impressive blocking and tackling skills.

9. By that time, he was about four feet taller than he had been at Gilbert Grunge, and the flab had turned into muscle.

10. Mimi decided that he was the light of her life, and Humpy and she were Homecoming King and Queen their senior year.

11. By then, Humpy was known as Hammer Hogroll, and he went to college on a football scholarship and then played for the Seattle Seahawks.

12. Ollie became a politician, still using the dodging and running techniques he learned from Humpy, aka Hammer, and wound up as the head of the IRS.

Go back and see how many compound nouns you can find, writing the word(s) after the sentence.

PARTS OF SPEECH

VERBS:

Definition: A word that shows **action** or state of being (the verb "be.".).

    Test: Is it something you can **do**? Can you _____?
        Ex: Can you walk, swim, exercise, hope, send, etc?

    Derivational Suffixes:
        -ize or -ise _____
        -ate_____
        -ify _____

Lexical Suffixes: -d, -ed, -n, -en, -t -ing. These endings show the tense of verbs.

    Remember, some verbs have irregular tense forms: go/went/gone.

Use in a sentence: Show what the subject is **doing.**

Position in a sentence: After the subject of a sentence or after the subject of a clause.

Types:
    Main Verb: The last verb in a verb phrase OR the **only** verb.

        Ex: Ollie must have <u>been</u> crazy.
            Elvira had <u>stepped</u> in a cow pie.
            Rancid <u>was</u> an old trapper.

    Helping (Auxiliary) Verb: Verb in front of the main verb.
        List of Helping Verbs –

See your Special Word Groups sheet.
You should LEARN these!

        Ex: Ollie <u>must have</u> been crazy.
            Elvira <u>had</u> stepped in a cow pie.

<u>Does</u> Elvira wish she had worn shoes?

Action Verb: A verb that shows **action.** (duh!)

>Ex: Ollie <u>catapulted</u> into the pond on his motorbike.

Linking Verb:
A verb that <u>links</u> the subject to a noun or adjective that <u>renames</u> or <u>describes</u> it.

>Ex: Ollie <u>became</u> airborne.
>Rancid <u>was</u> an old trapper.
>The cherry pie <u>looked</u> delicious.

List of Linking Verbs -- See your Special Word Groups sheet. You need to COMMIT THESE TO MEMORY FOREVER!!

Transitive/Intransitive Verbs:
Transitive verbs have a Direct Object in a sentence. Intransitive verbs don't.

(Don't stress about this; it'll make better sense when you study Parts of Sentences.)

Voice: Verbs are used in sentences in either the **active** or the **passive** Voice.

>In **Active Voice,** the subject of the sentence is doing (performing) the action of the verb:

>Ex: Scut Farkas *gave* me a swirly.

>In **Passive Voice,** the subject of the sentence is being acted upon:

>Ex: I *was given* a swirly by Scut Farkas

(Lest you think that the "by phrase" at the end of the sentence is a dead giveaway, sometimes it isn't there. Ex: I *was* the recipient of a swirly.)

Mood: Verbs also express **Mood:**

> **Indicative Mood:** The verb simply expresses a fact, an opinion, or a question. Ex: Water *is* wet. Water *feels* wonderful. *Does* your water *come* from a spring?
>
> **Imperative Mood:** The verb expresses a command or request. Ex: *Make* your bed. Please *bring* me a cookie. (Note that the subject of these sentences is understood to be "you.")
>
> **Subjunctive Mood:** The verb expresses a suggestion, a necessity, a wish, or a condition contrary to fact.
>
> Ex: It is very important that you *be* at the meeting.
>
> If I *were* you, I'd be careful. I wish I *were* a millionaire! If it *were* summer, I wouldn't be in school.

A Note on **Verb Tenses**:

Understanding and writing correct verb tenses is more a matter of **usage**, which we will deal with later. BUT, if you *must* know, here's a quick example:

Present Tense: I write
Past Tense: I wrote
Future Tense: I will write

Present Perfect Tense: I have written
Past Perfect Tense: I had written
Future Perfect Tense: I will have written

Present Progressive: I am writing
Past Progressive: I was writing
Future Progressive: I will be writing

Present Perfect Progressive: I have been writing
Past Perfect Progressive: I had been writing
Future Perfect Progressive: I will have been writing

Principal **P**arts of **V**erbs: base form, present participle, past, and past participle: write, (is) writing, wrote, (have) written

Tricksy Verbs:
Lie vs. lay, rise vs. raise, sit vs. set, and other irregular verbs can definitely be tricky to use. But that's the **Usage/Mechanics** thing again. Stay tuned! **Verbals** include gerunds, participles, and infinitives. They are not _used_ as verbs, so their discussion comes later too.

Verb Practice   Name _____

Directions: Underline all Verbs and Verb Phrases. Double underline Linking Verbs.

1. It seemed strange to the teacher that her students were so quiet when she walked into the room.

2. They all had their books out and were ready with pencils and paper.

3. The kids sat expectantly and waited for the teacher's instructions.

4. First, she called the names of all the students and took the attendance for the day.

5. Then she realized why it was so quiet.

6. Although it had never happened before, Phooter, Space, and Ollie were all absent.

7. Suddenly, the door opened, and Phooter walked in with a tardy slip.

8. Then Space made his appearance and shuffled to the teacher's desk, trying to look nonchalant as a few students snickered.

9. Last but not least, Ollie lurched through the door, stumbled over someone's backpack, and did a face plant on the floor.

10. By that time, the classroom decorum had deteriorated considerably, and it was awhile before they all settled down.

11. The teacher sighed, gave each of the three boys "the look," and started the lesson.

12. Things were definitely back to normal, the class reluctantly went to work, and the rest of the hour was like any other, certainly not boring.

PARTS OF SPEECH

ADVERBS:

Definition: A word that *modifies* (describes) a verb, adjective, or another adverb.
An adverb tells **where, when, how,** or to what extent.

Examples
walked <u>slowly</u>	(how)
walked <u>there</u>	(where)
<u>very</u> quickly	(to what extent)
<u>really</u> late	(to what extent)
<u>always</u> eats	(when)

Derivational Suffix: -ly is the mark of many adverbs; in fact you can often make an adjective into an adverb by adding -ly: bright--brightly/ loud--loudly

*Be careful! Some adjectives end in -ly too; friendly, likely, monthly, timely, manly, lovely, lonely, only, etc.

Lexical Suffixes: Like adjectives, adverbs have three forms of comparison, formed by adding *-er* and *-est* or by putting *more/most* in front: fast/faster/fastest colorfully/ more colorfully/ most colorfully.

Position in a Sentence: This is *important business* in determining whether an adverb modifies a verb, an adjective, or another adverb.

Here's the deal:

1. If an *adverb* modifies a **verb**, it can be *anywhere* in the sentence -- OR you can *move* it anywhere in the sentence!
Rancid <u>slowly</u> sneaked up on the weasel.
Rancid sneaked up on the weasel <u>slowly</u>.
<u>Slowly</u>, Rancid sneaked up on the weasel.

Negatives are a special group of adverbs that always modify verbs: no, not, -n't, never, etc.

2. If an adverb modifies an **adjective**, it will be *right in front of it!* You *can't* move it anywhere else in the sentence.
    Scut Farkas was very scary. *Scary* is an adjective describing Scut Farkas; *very* is an adverb modifying *scary*.
    Scut used extremely harsh tactics to keep us under his thumb.

    AND, the only adverbs that modify adjectives are in a Special Group of Adverbs called Intensifiers! These words include the following: very, too, so, really, quite, extremely, unusually, more, most, etc. Now you know that the "more" and "most" used in making comparisons are--**adverbs!**

3. If an adverb modifies another **adverb**, again it will *be in front of it* and you can't move it anywhere else:
    Scut attacked very sneakily, making him difficult to detect in advance. *Sneakily* is an adverb modifying the verb *attacked*, and *very* is an adverb modifying the adverb *sneakily*.

    AND AGAIN, the only adverbs that modify other adverbs are the Intensifiers. If the adverb is **not** an Intensifier, it ***has*** *to modify the verb!*

Practice with Linking Verbs   Name _____

Directions: Find and underline Linking Verbs in these sentences.

1. Today was Sunday, and I couldn't wait for dinner.

2. The fried chicken looked delicious, and it smelled wonderful.

3. The mashed potatoes were mounds of cloud-like goodness.

4. Rich gravy steamed in its bowl, and I was ready to eat.

5. My favorite piece of chicken is the drumstick, but I will eat wings too.

6. The coating tasted crunchy when I took a bite.

7. The meat was juicy and flavourful.

8. Five pieces of chicken and two helpings of potatoes and gravy were actually enough.

9. Mom passed the salad, but I told her I was full.

10. She also had fixed broccoli, but that sounded awful.

11. Four rolls tasted great, but I suddenly became extremely full.

12. I only had enough room for pie; it was apple.

13. Of course, I was really sleepy by then and had to take a nap.

14. I do love Sundays; they are awesome.

Adverb Practice   Name _____

Directions: Underline all adverbs and circle adverb intensifiers.

1. Phooter and Space didn't try to get into trouble; they just managed to do it really easily.

2. It was during the freshman class sex lecture that they totally fell apart.

3. The visiting nurse, a very nice lady who already knew how to deal with squirrelly teenagers, conducted the class during P.E.

4. In the first place, it was a serious mistake to have the two boys sitting so closely to each other.

5. The very first part of the class had to do with naming parts.

6. Phooter and Space did pretty well until a certain anatomical term was casually mentioned.

7. At that point, they completely cracked up.

8. Needless to say, the teacher immediately removed them from the premises and quickly sent them to the office.

9. They would have to endure private instruction during their lunch hour, which was too short anyway.

10. They managed to get through the ordeal but totally missed lunch.

11. They apologized later to the nurse and to the teacher, quite embarrassed that they had behaved so badly.

12. They sincerely promised they would stay out of trouble, at least for awhile.

Further Directions: Follow your teacher's instructions to show what word

The adverb or adverb intensifier modifies.

PARTS OF SPEECH

ADJECTIVES:

Definition: A word that *modifies* (describes) a noun or pronoun. *Modifies* means "changes/alters the meaning."
An adjective tells which **one, what kind, or how many.**

Examples:
<u>that</u> <u>fat</u> cat
<u>each</u> one
<u>blue</u> baboon
<u>several</u> others
<u>rare</u> air
twenty-one days
<u>her</u> Aunt Pat

Note that some adjectives may have been pronouns in a former life, **but**, the part of speech of a word depends on how it's used!

Derivational Suffixes:
... -ful _____
... -less _____
... -ous _____
... -al _____
... -ent/-ant _____
... -ic _____

Lexical Suffixes:
...-er / -est: These suffixes are used to make comparisons.

For example: pretty/prettier/prettiest young/younger/youngest.

Sometimes those endings won't work on an adjective -- beautiful/beautifuller/beautifullest?! So, you put <u>more</u> or <u>most</u> in front: beautiful/more beautiful/most beautiful

* For the seriously smart: the three forms of comparison are named the **positive**, the **comparative**, and the **superlative**.

Use and Position in a Sentence:

> **In front of** the noun they describe: <u>rare</u> bear
>
> **After** a linking verb:* they go back to describe the noun subject: That bear is <u>rare</u>. That cake tastes <u>fake.</u>
>
> * See **Special Word Groups** List

Kinds:

> Articles: **a, an, the**
>
> Demonstrative: this, that, these, those

You can make up some exercises for the three forms of comparison of adjectives. Just don't do what a former student did:

Ill   (<u>worse)</u> (<u>dead)</u> (!!)
Actually, it's ill, more ill, most ill.
Say these with a British accent or they won't sound right!

Exercises for Adjectives:

The positive form for each adjective is given. Write the comparative and superlative forms for each.

1. good   _____   _____

2. pretty   _____   _____

3. clear   _____   _____

4. beautiful   _____   _____

5. fun   _____   _____

6. comfortable   _____   _____

7. stupid   _____   _____

8. rare   _____   _____

9. blue   _____   _____

10. true   _____   _____

Write 10 sentences using an adjective after a Linking Verb.

Adjective Practice   Name _____

Directions: Underline the adjectives in these sentences; then draw an arrow to the word that the adjective modifies. Omit *a, an,* and *the.*

1. It was the great American Technicolor puke-off, and Phooter started it.

2. Everyone expected that since Phooter was known as a reliable gagger who could produce a puke at will.

3. The nervous teacher, Mr. Retched, was himself a great gagger although he tried to hide his sad affliction.

4. The awful smell was enough to infect Ollie with the dread disease, so he was the second puker to succumb.

5. Space followed with an amazing projectile puke, and by then it was time to vacate the whole area.

6. Some unfortunate students headed for the bathroom, and the others, whose green complexions were noticed by the P.E. students, huddled in the gym.

7. Fortunately the teacher's aide was able to maintain a semblance of control, and she headed for the janitor closet and some "Oops."

8. Unfortunately it was a toss-up concerning which of the two smells was the worse odor.

9. Mr. Retched had abandoned his sick students in favor of the teacher's lounge, a long way down the hall.

10. Finally, the better students filtered back into the empty classroom, and the rest of them followed.

11. Mr. R, however, had to leave the building and take a sick day; he would never teach that science unit again.

More Adjective Practice   Name _____

Underline the Adjectives in the following sentences. Don't forget to look for Adjectives after Linking Verbs too. Draw an arrow to the word modified. You may omit *a, an,* and *the*.

1. Phooter was good at irritating his father, even when he didn't realize he was being obnoxious.

2. He often worked with his dad and could make Mr. Fortner's eye twitch even before they got out of their short driveway.

3. He was talkative when his dad just wanted some morning silence.

4. Phooter was hardly ever quiet, and he chattered about football and hunting and snowmobiles until his dad started to look weary.

5. Phooter got to drive home from the logging job one day, and actually remained silent while Mr. Fortner napped.

6. Suddenly, Phooter slammed on the brakes, just to see if his father was alert.

7. Phooter was a great mimic and could do all kinds of different voices.

8. He even had special voices for the family pets and held imaginary conversations between their two dogs.

9. Mr. Fortner finally had enough one evening and hollered, "Dogs can't talk!"

10. Of course Phooter thought that remark was hysterical and could not stop laughing.

11. It is a good thing that the two of them really do like each other, do fun things together, and do remain friendly.

PARTS OF SPEECH

PREPOSITIONS:

Definition: A word that shows a relationship between two nouns in a sentence. For example: The squirrel is **on** the log. The preposition **on** shows the relationship between the squirrel and the log.

The squirrel can be … **by** the log, **beside** the log, **above** the log, **below** the log, **with** the log, **in** the log, etc. In fact, the squirrel can even be said to be **of** the log, if he lives there, just as you can be said to be **of** UpRiver School!

Examples: See your Special Word Groups sheet! You need to be able to ID them!

Use: Prepositions are used to begin **prepositional phrases**, which start with a preposition and end with a noun or pronoun, called *the object of the preposition.*

Adjectives may, of course, be between the preposition and its object and are part of the phrase:
 … **in** the dark and stormy night
 … **beside** the moonlit lake
 … **throughout** the long lecture

Prepositional phrases are used as **adjectives** or **adverbs** in a sentence.

If used as an **adjective,** the prepositional phrase will *follow* the **noun** it describes:

The bow season <u>for elk</u> opens early.
Hunters <u>in camouflage</u> get up before dawn.
All <u>of the hunters</u> hope they will be lucky.

If used as an **adverb,** the prepositional phrase can modify a **verb,** an **adjective,** or another **adverb:**

If it modifies a **verb**, the prepositional phrase is *moveable*:

<u>In the evening</u> I have homework.
I have homework <u>in the evening</u>.

If it modifies an **adjective**, it will be right after it:

I am happy <u>without any</u>.

If it modifies an **adverb**, it will be right after it.

The girl paints well <u>for a beginner</u>.

A *bare*, *naked* preposition (one without an object, all alone, by itself) is an **adverb**:
Don't look <u>down.</u>
Ollie tipped <u>over.</u>

* The object of a preposition is <u>never</u> one of the main parts of a sentence!! It can't be a subject, predicate noun, direct object or indirect object.

**REMEMBER THE SQUIRREL AND THE LOG!!!

Preposition Practice   Name _____

Directions: Find and underline the prepositional phrases in the following sentences.

1. Since the day of their births, Phooter and Ollie have been the best of friends.

2. Before the time they could even talk, they made motor noises like chainsaws, motorcycles, and snowmobiles.

3. After that, they played logging in the yard for hours at a time.

4. They went to preschool and sat together during "graduation" at the Presbyterian Church.

5. At one point, they had to reach under their seats to get hats for a musical number, accidentally bumping heads.

6. For some unknown reason, they thought that was just hysterical, and the situation deteriorated from there.

7. By the time the festivities were over, Phooter's mom, Mrs. Fortner, was furious at them.

8. The next day, she called the principal at Gilbert Grunge Grammar School.

9. She called Mrs Gravity promptly at 8 o'clock in the morning.

10. "If you had been a witness to preschool graduation last night, you'd know why I'm requesting that Phooter and Ollie NOT be in the same kindergarten class next!" she said.

PARTS OF SPEECH

CONJUNCTIONS:

Definition: "Conjunction Junction, what's your function? Hookin' up words and phrases and clauses!" (Your teacher can sing this little song to you!)

Types:

Coordinating: Remember **FANBOY:** for, and, nor, but, or, yet. You need to memorize these **conjunctions** as they are *very important in punctuation!*

Coordinating conjunctions join items that are the *same*: nouns, prepositional phrases, sentences, etc. This is the principle concerning a very important writing rule -- **parallel structure!** More later about that.

> Examples: He rode down the driveway, over the bank, and into the pond.
> The students were rude, crude, and unattractive.
> Ollie is inattentive, yet he is happy.

Correlative: These are *pairs* of conjunctions that also join items that are the *same*. Again, they are important in **punctuation** and **parallel structure.** They include these "double" conjunctions: *either...or, neither...nor, both...and, not only...but (also), whether...or.*

> Examples: *Both* Scut Farkas *and* his gang struck fear into our hearts.
> *Either* Scut would enforce his reign of terror, *or* one of his henchmen would do it.
> Scut was *not only* mean *but also* ugly.

* A Note on "for:" When *for* is a conjunction, it connects clauses and means "because."

Ex: I waited *for* Cholmondeley (pronounced "Chumly"), *for* I was sure he would arrive shortly. (Rather a British-sounding thing, don't you think? Most Americans really don't use *for* much as a conjunction.)

Otherwise, *for* is a preposition (as is the first *for* in the Cholmondelay sentence.): Our teacher told us to study *for* the test. We waited *for* the last possible moment. We were sorry *for* our bad grades on the English test.

Subordinating: These conjunctions are listed on your Special Word Groups Sheet under "Subordinators." They introduce subordinate clauses, about which you will learn later!

Conjunctive Adverbs: These important words are listed on your Special Word Groups Sheet under "Sentence Connectors." That's what they do--connect sentences. You will need to know about them for punctuation and matters of writing style!

STAY TUNED!!!

PARTS OF SPEECH

INTERJECTIONS:

Definition: "IN-TER-JEC-TIONS show emotion or excitement!" They really don't relate grammatically to any of the other words in a sentence.

Punctuation: They are usually set off by an exclamation mark. Sometimes, they are just set off by a comma.

Examples:

>Beans! I just can't seem to find my pet tarantula.
>
>Good grief! Why did you scare her under the couch?
>
>Aha, there she is, good old Sybil.
>
>Chocolate!

Common interjections: oh, wow, well, aw, yes, great, etc.
>Actually, almost any word could be an interjection.

Note: Interjections are common in **informal** speaking and writing. They should not, however, be used in formal situations unless they are part of written dialogue.

PRONOUNS: (Yep, it's the lowdown on the pronoun.)

>Definition: a word that takes the place of a noun in a sentence …
>as a subject: *He* is a nerd.
>… as a predicate noun: The tests are *those* in the box.
>… as a direct object: The teacher passed *them* out.
>… as an indirect object: The test gave *me* hives.
>… as the object of a preposition: The test had hard questions on *it*.
>
>Use: a pronoun can be used any way a noun is used in a sentence **or** as an adjective. It may also be used to introduce certain groups of words.

Ex: She is my best friend. *She* is used as a noun subject. *My* is used as an adjective describing friend.

Ex: Some of the apples that I picked have a few worms. *Some* is used as the noun subject, *that* introduces a relative clause, and *few* is used as an adjective.

Kinds:

Personal Pronouns: refer to a person or persons:
First Person: I, me, my, mine, we, us, our, ours.
Second Person: you, your, yours
Third Person: he, him, his, she, her, hers, it, its, they, them, their, theirs.

Reflexive/Intensive Pronouns:
First Person: myself, ourselves
Second Person: yourself, yourselves
Third Person: himself, herself, itself, themselves

Reflexive: refers to a noun/pronoun earlier in sentence.
Ex: The students considered *themselves* brilliant. She is *herself* again.

Intensive: Emphasizes a noun/pronoun.
Ex: Rancid *himself* pulled the trigger.
I *myself* saw him do it.

Demonstrative Pronouns: point out nouns.
This, that, these, those

Interrogative Pronouns: introduce a question.
What, which, who, whom, whose

Relative Pronouns: introduce a group of words called a Relative Clause.
Who, whom, whose, which, that
Ex: *who* was my best friend
whom I saw yesterday
that I missed

Indefinite Pronouns: so-called when used as nouns. (Otherwise, these words are adjectives!)
See your SPECIAL WORD GROUPS LIST to find out what these are!!

HINT: all, both, each, some, any, one, etc!!

IMPORTANT NOTE ABOUT PRONOUNS:
Actually, there is no such thing as a **pronoun** because they're *used* as either nouns or adjectives!

REMEMBER WHEN YOU ARE IDENTIFYING PARTS OF SPEECH THAT IT DEPENDS ON HOW THE WORD IS USED IN THE SENTENCE!!!

Ex: The *moon* came out from behind the clouds. *Moon* = noun
Some strange people used to wear *moon* boots. *Moon* = adjective
Both of the girls wore curlers. *Both* = noun
Both girls wore curlers. *Both* = adjective

Information for the seriously smart: 99.9% of all the words in the English language are **nouns, verbs, adjectives, or adverbs**!
(The rest are **prepositions** (about 60), **conjunctions** (about 14), or **interjections** (about 15)! Recall that **pronouns** are really **nouns** or **adjectives**!

Some teachers feel that pronouns should be taught after nouns, verbs, adjectives, and adverbs because they are a "special" case and used as *other* parts of speech. It's up to you whether or not you move them there. They follow nouns in this presentation since they are closely related.

Pronoun Practice   Name _____

Directions: Underline each Pronoun and draw an arrow to its Antecedent.

1. Phooter Fortner and Space Saptree were pretty good buddies, and both of them liked football a lot.

2. The boys went to football camp every summer, and they couldn't wait for practice to start for the fall season.

3. Practice was tough, but it was a lot of fun, and the boys really got themselves in shape.

4. When the first game day finally arrived, the boys were nervous but excited, and they got to the field really early.

5. Space had eaten three helpings of tater tot casserole, and they made him so full he hoped that he wouldn't throw up.

6. Phooter did throw up, but then he felt better and gleefully tackled his mom on the couch before he left for the game.

7. Mrs. Fortner was caught unaware, but she managed to recover quickly.

8. Mr. Fortner, however, yelled at Phooter and told him to settle down.

9. The boys took two chainsaws to the game so that they could rev them up when the Lumberjacks ran onto the field.

10. The coach made the boys take the chains out so that the principal wouldn't have a fit worrying about safety issues.

11. Soon the game would finally be underway, and it would be a good one.

PRONOUNS

PERSONAL

I, me, my, mine

you, your, yours

he, him, his

she, her, hers

it, its

we, us, our, ours

they, them, their, theirs

REFLEXIVE/INTENSIVE

myself	ourselves
yourself	yourselves
himself	themselves
herself	
itself	

RELATIVE

who	whom
whose	which
that	

INTERROGATIVE

whom

which

what

whose

DEMONSTRATIVE

this

that

these

those

INDEFINITE

all	everyone	none	another
everything	no one	any	few
one	more	some	both
most	somebody	each	someone
much	someone	either	neither
such	everybody	nobody	anybody
many	several	anyone	

SPECIAL WORD GROUPS LIST

Helping Verbs

Am	has	should
Is	have	would
Are	had	may
Was	do	might
Were	does	must
Be	did	can
Being	shall	could
Been	will	

Linking Verbs

am	look	seem
is	sound	become
are	taste	remain
was	smell	appear
were	feel	grow*
be		stay*
being		
been		

Conjunctions (Coordinate)

And but or nor
for (when it means because)
Yet so

Relatives (pronouns)

who whom whose which that

Sentence Connectors (Conjunctive Adverbs)

However	therefore
Furthermore	moreover
Nevertheless	consequently
Otherwise	thus
Indeed	in fact

Subordinators (Subordinate Conjunctions)

before**	after**
since**	until**
when	if
as	while
because	unless
although	though
whenever	wherever
	so that

Prepositions				Intensifiers
About	behind	against	because of	(adverbs)
At	for	between	according to	very really
Down	across	in		quite too
Of	on	past		extremely
Since**	until**	toward		so
Before**	after**	within		more most
Above	below	among		
From	by	during		articles
Over	into	off		a
To	around	through		an
With	under	up		the
Like	without	upon		

Special Word Groups

Notes:

* *Grow* and *stay* are **linking verbs** only if followed by an adjective. Ex: He grew old. (LV) He grew a garden. (Action Verb).

** *Before, after, since,* and *until* are subordinators when followed by a whole sentence. They are prepositions if followed by a noun phrase.

Ex: Before I got up ... (before = subordinator); Before the dance ... (before = preposition.)

Note that *because* is always a subordinator; *because of* is a preposition.

ALL WORDS NOT ON THIS LIST ARE EITHER
NOUNS, VERBS, ADJECTIVES, OR ADVERBS!!

Parts of Speech Exercise   Name _____

Directions: Identify the nouns, verbs, and adjectives in the following excerpt. You should have 11 of them. All the other words are on the Special Word Groups List. Have Fun!!

From "Jabberwocky" by Lewis Carroll

'Twas brillig, and the slithy toves

Did gyre and gimble in the wabe.

All mimsy were the borogroves,

And the mome raths outgrabe.

Helpful hints: Think of words that might substitute for the "nonsense" words that would make sense to you. That will help you identify the part of speech!

    Example: The tinky delves were mooshy.

    The little birds were beautiful.

    tinky = adjective (y ending like tiny, shiny, briny)

    delves = noun (plural s ending, follows adj.)

    mooshy = adjective (predicated adjective
               following linking verb, y ending)

Parts of Speech Practice

Follow your teacher's directions for this worksheet.

1. Phooter Fortner and Ollie Hopnoggin had been friends forever.

2. They managed to get into a fair amount of trouble in the twelve years they had been together.

3. They both loved to ride dirt bikes and snowmobiles.

4. They also loved hunting, fishing, camping, and logging.

5. They spent their summers logging with Phooter's dad and Ollie's grandpa.

6. Phooter loved playing football and watching the Seattle Seahawks.

7. Ollie couldn't tell a first down from a fumble, but he played too.

8. At least when school started, there was football and hunting to look forward to.

9. They weren't all that crazy about school.

Parts of Speech Paragraph   Name _____

Directions: Identify parts of speech as directed:

   Let me begin by saying that I don't hold with lying, a disgusting habit. After a lifetime spent in the company of elk hunters, I am pleased to report that they hate lying as much as I do. It's true that elk hunters are human and that an occasional lie may escape their lips while they are relaxing around the campfire of an evening. A hunter might just describe his packing of an elk quarter up a steep hill more like carrying a refrigerator up the Matterhorn, but that is an exaggeration to be forgiven. Changing a five-point rack to an eight-point rack is unforgivable, an outright lie. It is permissible only to add only two points at most to a rack, but that is only for a hunter's first elk. After they have been shot, his future elk are not allowed to grow any points at all. The exception is if the hunter has reached the age of sixty-five; then anything goes. I know an elk hunter who gave up the sport when he reached sixty-five. After I saw him a month later, he had bagged at least a dozen more elk than I was aware of, which was three.

Note to Teacher: This paragraph also works as a Punctuation Practice. Just delete the punctuation and instruct the students to number for each sentence and write the rule!

Parts of Speech Review -- Cheat Sheet for Your Brain!

NOUNS: Name a person, place, thing, or idea.

    Example: Mr. Andersen (person) is the principal (person) of our school (thing), and he (pronoun/noun) gives us (pronoun/noun) encouragement (idea).

VERBS: Show action or state of being. The **main verb** in a sentence is the *last* or *only* verb.

    Helping Verbs are found *in front of* the main verb and listed on your Special Word Groups sheet.

    Linking Verbs link the subject of the sentence to a noun or adjective that *renames* or *describes* the subject. See Special Word Groups sheet.

    Examples: Mr. Andersen can be (helping verbs) found (main verb) in the math classroom or in the office.

    He is (linking verb) a good teacher and a good principal.

    He also talks (main verb) really fast!

ADJECTIVES: Tell which one, what kind, or how many. They describe nouns and come in front of them or after a linking verb.

    Examples: Mr. Andersen is not only a fast (what kind) talker but a nice (what kind) guy.

    Several (how many) things could happen to those (which ones) students who are troublesome (predicate adjective). None of them are good (predicate adjective).

They often end up in <u>Mr. Andersen's</u> (proper adjective!) office!

ADVERBS: Tell how, when, or where. Can be anyplace in a sentence and describe the verb.

Examples: <u>Slowly</u> (how he walked) the unruly student walked to the office.
The student walked <u>slowly</u> (how) to the office.
The boy walked to the office <u>slowly</u> (how).
He was <u>never</u> (when) in trouble and wanted to run <u>away</u> (where).

CONJUNCTIONS: Join words or groups of words: and, but, or, nor, for (because), yet, so.

Examples: He was relieved <u>and</u> happy when Mr. Andersen wasn't mean <u>or</u> unreasonable, <u>but</u> he decided to be a good kid from then on.

PREPOSITIONS: Show a relationship between two nouns, like "the squirrel and the log."

See your Special Word Groups sheet.

Example: The students <u>of</u> UpRiver school <u>in</u> Fernwood come <u>from</u> the St. Maries River area <u>around</u> Santa, Fernwood, and Emida and learn <u>about</u> the world <u>outside</u> Idaho.

Sentences

COMPLETE/INCOMPLETE SENTENCES:

To be a Complete Sentence, a group of words must have a **subject** and a **verb** and **express a complete thought**. Otherwise, it's a **Fragment**.

Examples:

	Complete:	Scut was contemplating his next act of terrorism.
	Fragment:	While Scut was contemplating his next act of terrorism…
		Contemplating his next act of terrorism…
	Complete:	Hortense adjusted her horn-rimmed spectacles and gave me a look of disgust.
	Fragment:	After Hortense adjusted her horn-rimmed spectacles…
	Complete:	Who was that masked man?
	Fragment:	Whose eyes were like burning coals…
	Complete:	I knew that it was Ollie Hopnoodle.
	Fragment:	That it was Ollie Hopnoodle…

WARNING: Writing incomplete sentences is totally against the law and causes English teachers to throw **slobbering fits!**

SUBJECTS AND PREDICATES:

The **simple** subject of a sentence is the noun/pronoun the sentence is about. The **complete** subject includes all adjectives and prepositional phrases that go with it.

> <u>One</u> of my best friends was my pet blacksnake George.
> <u>One</u> is the **simple** subject.
> <u>One of my best friends</u> is the **complete** subject.

The **simple** predicate of a sentence is the verb or verb phrase (that includes helping verbs). The **complete** predicate includes the verb or verb phrase and everything that goes after it.

> George <u>measured</u> about five feet long in his stocking feet.
> <u>Measured</u> is the **simple** predicate.
> George measured about five feet long in his stocking <u>feet.</u> All that underlined stuff is the complete predicate.

You can generally divide sentences into their two parts right in front of the verb or verb phrase. Be careful with questions as the verb phrase may be split, with part at the beginning of the sentence: Did Mabel staple and fold all the letters?

<u>Mabel</u> is the simple (and complete) subject. <u>Did staple and</u> fold all those letters is the complete predicate. (Staple and <u>fold</u> is the simple predicate.)

ANYWAY, how big a deal you need to make out of this **complete** subject and predicate stuff depends on your teacher and testing requirements!

TYPES OF SENTENCES:

Declarative: A declarative sentence makes a *statement*, states a *fact*. It ends with a *period*.
Example: My pet tarantula's name is Sybil.

Interrogative: An interrogative sentence asks a *question*. It ends with a *question mark*..
Example: Do you have a pet tarantula?

Imperative: An imperative sentence makes a *request* or *command*. It usually ends with a period but could end with an exclamation mark -- if it's commanding enough!

    Example: Don't sit on that tarantula!
                Please put Sybil in her cage.
                 Do your homework.
                 Stop!

Important Note: The subject of an imperative sentence is understood to be "you."
(You) don't sit on that tarantula.
(You) do your homework.
(You) stop!

Exclamatory: An exclamatory sentence shows feeling, emotion, or excitement. It ends with an exclamation mark.
Example: How confused we are!
               What an exciting lesson this is!

PARTS OF SENTENCES:

Subject: Ask yourself **who** or **what** the sentence is about!

How to Find the Subject of a Sentence:

1. Cross out all **prepositional phrases!** The subject of a sentence is **never** in a prepositional phrase. Remember "the squirrel and the log!" Look at your Special Word Groups Sheet!

2. The subject is usually the **first** noun or pronoun in the sentence.

3. If the sentence is a question (interrogative), turn it into a statement (declarative.)

    Ex: Was Rancid late for the hunting trip?
    <u>Rancid</u> was late for the hunting trip.

4. If the sentence is a request or command (imperative), (you) is the understood subject.

    Ex: Clean your room.
    (<u>You</u>) clean your room.

5. The subject of a sentence can be at the end.

    Ex: Diving for cover were Zach and Jess.
    <u>Zach and Jess</u> were diving for cover.
    How surprised we were!
    <u>We</u> were how surprised!

6. The subject of a sentence can be **compound,** that is, include two or more nouns joined by a conjunction.

    Ex: <u>Jesse, Zach, and Ollie</u> took off on their dirt bikes.

Verb: The <u>verb or verb phrase</u> tells what the subject is **doing!** (It can also tell what it **is.** See Forms of the verb "**Be.**")

    Ex: Retch Sweeney <u>was packing</u> his gear for hunting camp.
    He <u>would meet</u> Rancid Crabtree at Bud's at 4:00 a.m.
    Rancid <u>was</u> the best hunter in the Northwest.

Locating the verb **first** is probably the best way to find the **subject!** Find the verb; then ask, "**who** or **what**_____?" The answer will be the subject!

> Ex: Melba Peachbottom was the loveliest girl at Delmore Blight Junior High School.
> Verb: was
> **Who** or **what** *was?* Melba Peachbottom = subject
>
> Stink Miller trapped skunks in his spare time.
> Verb: *trapped*
> **Who** or **what** *trapped?* Stink Miller = subject.

Compound verbs: Remember, like subjects, the verb may be made up of more than one verb/verb phrase.

> Ex: Stink trapped skunks, hung around Retch Sweeney, and skipped school for a living.
>
> Verb: *trapped, hung, skipped*
> **Who** trapped, hung, and skipped? Stink = subject

SENTENCE PATTERNS:

S - V: Some sentences are complete with just a subject and a verb. Those are **S**ubject - **V**erb sentence patterns.

> Ex: I was talking to Olga Bonemarrow about our Science project.
> Verb = was talking
> Subject = I

Remember to **cross out all prepositional phrases** when you are trying to figure out Sentence Patterns. They're just used as adjectives or adverbs and are **never** part of the Sentence Pattern!

> **Action/Linking Verbs:** Once you have located the subject and verb of the sentence, you need to identify the verb as an **action verb** or a **linking verb!**
>
> **Linking Verbs:** These verbs include the Forms of Be; the verbs of your senses: look, smell, taste, feel, sound; seem, become, remain, appear, grow*, and stay.* Special Word Groups Sheet!!

S - LV - SC: Subject - Linking Verb - Subject Complement:

> If the verb is **linking**, a *subject complement* will finish the sentence pattern. The *subject complement* will be one of two things:
>
> **Predicate Noun (nominative):** follows a linking verb (usually a form of the verb "Be") and **re-names/means the same** as the subject.

> > Ex: Olga was my lab partner.
> > Subject = Olga
> > Linking Verb = was
> > Predicate Noun = partner
> > (Olga and partner are the **same**.)
> >
> > Ex: Olga became a nurse after college.
> > Subject = Olga
> > Linking Verb = became
> > Predicate Noun = nurse

Predicate Adjective: follows a Linking Verb and **describes** the subject.

> Ex: Olga was intelligent and sympathetic.
> Subject = Olga
> Linking Verb = was
> Predicate Adjective=intelligent and sympathetic (Notice it's *compound. Any* part of a sentence can be compound.)

> Ex: That cream cheese huckleberry pie looks scrumptious!
> Subject = pie
> Linking Verb = looks
> Predicate Adjective = scrumptious

** A Note on *grow**and *stay**: These verbs are **linking--if** followed by a noun re-naming the subject or an adjective describing the subject: Rancid grew old before his time. *Grew* is linking here because *old* describes Rancid. Rancid always grew a garden. *Grew* is **not** linking because garden doesn't rename Rancid.

S - V - DO: Action verbs are sometimes followed by a noun or pronoun that **receives** the action of the verb. NOTE that the verbs in this pattern are **not** linking verbs and that the **DO** is totally different from the **Subject**, unlike a **PN** that is the **same** as the subject noun.

> Ex: Unfortunately, I accidentally hit Olga with a flying fish during one of our science experiments.
> Verb = hit (**not** linking)
> Subject = I (what or who hit)
> Direct Object = Olga (I hit whom?) "I" and "Olga" are **different**

> Ex: Olga whacked me with her science book.
> Verb = whacked
> Subject = Olga (who whacked?)
> Direct Object = me (Olga whacked whom?)

S - V - IO - DO: In this sentence pattern, there is a **receiver** of the **direct object**, called the **indirect object**. It is a noun or pronoun always *in front of* the **direct object** and *different from* the **direct object** as well as *from* the **subject**.

Ex: Olga gave me a lump about the size of an orange.
Verb = gave
Subject = Olga
Direct Object = lump (what Olga gave)
Indirect Object = me (receiver of lump!)
Olga, lump, and me are all **different.**

Ex: Mrs. S. gave both of us detention.
Verb = gave
Subject = Mrs. S.
Direct Object = detention (what she gave)
Indirect Object = both (who got detention)
Nouns are **different.**

***Only for the seriously scholarly:** One more sentence pattern is fairly rare; in fact, most teachers don't even mention it, like until your junior year. It is **Subject - Verb - Object Complement - Direct Object.**

Only one kind of verb is ever in this pattern, including these and some similar ones: elect, chose, consider, name, think, believe, etc., and **only** if they are followed by two *nouns* that refer to the **same** person or thing **or** a *noun* followed by an *adjective* **describing** the noun.

Ex: We elected Retch Sweeney our class president.
Subject = We
Verb = elected
Direct Object = Retch Sweeny (We elected whom?)
Object Complement = president (We elected Retch Sweeney **(to be _____?)**
Note that Retch and <u>president</u> refer to the **same** thing!)

Ex: The class considered Retch capable up to a point.
Subject = class
Verb = considered
Direct Object = Retch
Object Complement = capable (Class considered Retch **to be _____?)**
Note that <u>capable</u> is an **adjective describing** Retch!

So, an **Object Complement is** like a Subject Complement since it can be either a *noun/pronoun* **re-naming** the noun in front of it **or** an *adjective* **describing** the noun in front of it! Cool, huh!

(If this is too much for you, just put your hands over your ears and sing, "Meow, meow, meow, meow; Meow, meow, meow, meow ...")!!!

•

Phrases, Clauses, And Clusters

PREPOSITIONAL PHRASES (Revisited)

Review Prepositional Phrases from the Parts of Speech section as/if your teacher directs.

VERBALS and VERBAL PHRASES

    PARTICIPLES and PARTICIPIAL PHRASES:

        PARTICIPLES are -ING or -ED verbs that are used Not as **verbs** but as **adjectives!**

            Ex: The *singing* canary was yellow. The *drowned* rat looked *disgusting* (predicate adjective). The *writing* assignment was late. Ollie had a *delayed* reaction.

        PARTICIPIAL PHRASES: Sometimes, the participle is expanded into a **participial phrase:**

            Ex: *Singing in the shower,* my brother drove us crazy. (Modifies "brother.")

                  Delayed by the eruption of Mount St. Helens, the mail was days late. (Modifies "mail.")

                  The pickup was a wreck, *totaled in the crash.* (Modifies "pickup.")

NOTE: Participial Phrases are also called **verb clusters**, set off from a sentence with **a comma.**

USAGE NOTE: Do **NOT** dangle your participles!! Always put them next to the word they modify!

        Ex: Having warned them in advance, the students were instructed by the teacher to re-write the paragraph. Dang participle!! The students didn't issue the warning!

Correct: Having warned them in advance, the teacher instructed the students to re-write the paragraph.

GERUNDS and GERUND PHRASES

GERUNDS are -ing verb forms that are used as *nouns*.

Ex: <u>Swimming</u> is really good exercise. (Noun subject.)

Rancid's profession was <u>hunting.</u> (Predicate Noun.)

You should give <u>wrestling</u> a try. (Indirect Object.)

Retch enjoys <u>hiking.</u> (Direct Object.)

He swept the sidewalk after <u>mowing.</u> (Object of the preposition "after.")

GERUND PHRASES consist of a gerund and any modifiers or complements it has. Since a gerund is a *verb* form it could have a complement (object).

Ex: <u>Baking wedding cakes</u> is Bertha's specialty. (Subject. "Cakes" is actually the direct object of "baking!" "Baking" what? "Cakes." Cool, huh?

<u>Barbecuing on the grill</u> is Dad's specialty. (Subject.)

We got into trouble for <u>talking in class.</u> (Object of the Preposition "for.")

We enjoyed <u>the rocking of the boat.</u> (Direct Object.)

NOTE TO TEACHER:

Sometimes students can confuse a gerund with a present participle used as part of the verb:

Ex: The deer was sniffing the wind before stepping into the meadow. The verb is "was sniffing." Makes no sense to say "sniffing the wind" is a gerund 'cause that would make it a predicate noun, and it doesn't re-name deer! "...stepping into the meadow" is, of course, a gerund phrase used as the object of the preposition "before."

When a noun or pronoun comes immediately before a gerund, use the possessive form of the noun or pronoun.

>Ex: <u>Jodi's cooking</u> is wonderful. (S)
>Nothing interrupts <u>our eating</u>. (DO)

INFINITIVES and INFINITIVE PHRASES

INFINITIVES: An **infinitve** is the word *to* plus a *verb*. ("To" plus a noun is a prepositional phrase, remember?) An **infinitive** can be used as a *Noun*, an *adjective*, or an *adverb* (Don't faint!! It's easy to tell!)

Ex: To study is usually a good idea. (Noun subject. The infinitive is part of the Sentence Pattern.)

Melba Peachbottom likes to study. (Noun direct object - part of sentence.)

The best time to study is early. (Adjective. It follows and describes the noun in front of it.)

Some students are not ready to study. (Adverb modifying the predicate adjective right in front of it.)

The horse ran to the stream to drink. (Adverb modifying the verb "ran," tells why. Could be moved to the beginning of the sentence and set off with a comma: To drink, the horse ran to the stream.

INFINITIVE PHRASE: Again, adjectives, prepositional phrases, and/or complements (objects) can be included:

Ex: To study for Mrs. S's English test is a good idea.
(Noun subject. Note that the infinitive phrase goes clear to the verb!)
Melba Peachbottom likes to study for hours at a time.
(Noun direct object.)

The best time to study English is early. (Adjective.)
Some students are never ready to study anything.
(Adverb modifying adjective "ready.")

The horse ran to the stream to drink water thirstily. (Adverb - tells why. Note that "to the stream is, indeed, a prepositional phrase!)

USAGE NOTE: Do NOT **split infinitives!** Don't put an adverb between the "to" and the verb!!

Ex: Retch needs to really try hard to bring his grades up next quarter. SPLIT INFINITIVE!!

Correction: **Move** the adverb! Retch needs <u>to try</u> really hard to bring his grades up next quarter.

HELPFUL HINTS:

Participles and participial phrases can be <u>crossed out,</u> and you still have a sentence pattern (complete sentence)!

Gerunds are part of the sentence and **can't** be crossed out to leave a complete sentence!

(The exception is a gerund or gerund phrase used as the object of a preposition, and then you just cross out the whole prepositional phrase as usual)

If an infinitive phrase is used as an adjective or adverb, you can cross it out and still have a sentence pattern (complete sentence)! If it's a noun, you **can't!**

APPOSITIVES: An **appositive** is a phrase that follows and **renames** a **noun.** Commas are usually used with appositives. An exception would be in the case of a single-word appositive.

> Examples: Retch Sweeney, <u>an old trapper</u>, was my idol.
>
> > My idol, a man who loved to eat, favored "sammiches."
> >
> > My brother Stinky loved to tag along.

ADJECTIVE PHRASES: An **adjective phrase** that starts with a *true* adjective (one that has three forms, like <u>rare, rarer, rarest</u>) is called a **Verb Cluster** (VC) and is set off from a sentence with a comma or commas.

> Examples: Retch saw a "double-breasted sapsucker," <u>rare and elusive</u>.
>
> > <u>Sharper than the edge of town</u>, Rancid pointed out an "iggle."
> >
> > My favorite bird, bigger than those two, is a "poop-a-quart."

CLAUSES: A **clause** is a group of words that contains a **subject** and a **verb**.

There are **two** kinds:

Independent Clause: An **independent clause** has a subject and a verb and expresses a complete thought. It can stand alone as a sentence; in fact it is a **sentence** or **sentence pattern**.

>   Example: Retch's feet ran furiously in empty space.
>   Ketchum Scritch held him up by his collar.

Dependent Clause: A **dependent clause** has a subject and a verb but does **not** expressa complete thought. It **cannot** stand alone as a sentence.

>   Example: Because Retch's feet ran furiously in empty space ...
>
>   Who held him up by his collar ...
>
>   Whatever Retch thought ...

Kinds of Dependent Clauses:

>   **Subordinate Clause** (SC): Begins with a **subordinator**, also called a *subordinate conjunction*—
>   see Special Word Groups Sheet for a list of subordinators
>
>   A **subordinate clause** is used as an **adverb**.
>
>   >   Examples:
>   >
>   >   Because Retch's feet ran furiously in empty space, he was getting nowhere fast.
>   >
>   >   Ketchum let him down after Retch's face turned an amazing color.
>
>   **Relative Clause** (RC): Begins with a **relative** (relative pronoun).
>
>   See Special Word Groups sheet.
>   A relative clause is used as an **adjective**.
>
>   >   Examples:

Ketchum, <u>who held Retch up by his collar</u>, dropped him like a hot rock.

Retch, <u>whose face was puce,</u> gasped for air.

It was the first time <u>that I saw him run</u>.

NOTE: Subordinate and Relative Clauses are always found **in addition** to the sentence pattern. You can cross them out and still have a complete sentence. Sometimes subordinate and relative clauses are set off by a comma or commas and sometimes not. You will learn about that when you study **punctuation!**

Noun Clause: A **noun clause** is a *dependent clause* that is used in place of a **noun** in a sentence. It is **never** set off by a comma or commas because it's **part of the sentence pattern!** It will be a subject, direct object, object of the preposition, predicate noun, or indirect object. You **can't** cross it out and still have a **complete sentence!**

Examples:

<u>That Ketchum was angry</u> was obvious. (Subject.)

He must have thought <u>that we had too many fish.</u> (Direct object.)

He always looks for <u>whoever he can catch breaking game laws</u>. (Object of the preposition.)

He always gave <u>whoever he caught</u> a ticket. (Indirect object.)

It really wasn't <u>what he thought</u>. (Predicate noun.)

PUNCTUATION

Conjunctions, Sentence Connectors, Two Sentence Patterns

1. **Series Rule** – In a series of three or more words or phrases with the last two joined by a conjunction, place a comma after each item, including one in front of the conjunction. _____, _____, c _____

    c = conjunction (and, but, or, nor, for yet, so)

Examples: Tom, Dick, and Harry are my brothers.

    The elk ran down the ridge, across the road, and into the timber.

    The class took the test, handed it in, and waited for the bell.

2. **SP, c SP.** – If a conjunction joins **two complete sentence patterns**, put a **comma** in front of the conjunction. Do **not** use a comma between two words or phrases that are not complete sentence patterns.

Examples: Students attended classes, and then they went to the gym for a Pep assembly.

    Students attended classes and a pep assembly. (No comma!)

    We drove to town, and we saw a movie.

    We drove to town and saw a movie. (No comma!)

3. **SP; sc SP.** – When two sentence patterns are joined by a **sentence connector**, put a **semicolon** in front of it. (A comma may be used after the **sc**.)

    sc = sentence connector (however, moreover, nevertheless, indeed otherwise, consequently, furthermore, thus, therefore, etc.)

Examples: Anne studied very hard; therefore she got an A.

Mary didn't study; consequently, she got a low grade.

4. **SP; SP.** – Two sentence patterns must be joined by a semicolon if they are in the same sentence and there are no connecting words.

Examples: Black often symbolizes death; red represents love.

The plot is simple; the theme is obscure.

NOTE: Conjunctions and sentence connectors are, of course, on the Special Word Groups list.

NOTE TO TEACHER: In journalistic writing, the comma in front of the conjunction joining the last two items in a series of three or more is omitted. That convention apparently harks back to the days of typesetting by hand and eliminated that step. Strunk and White's <u>Elements of Style</u> does support the use of the comma in front of the conjunction in a series.

Punctuation Worksheet 1

Punctuate the sentences correctly.

RULE: _____

1. My family and I went on horseback trips fished in the Joe slept under the stars and got home before the storm arrived.

2. Darcy Tara Dawn and Lena all miss Shelly's help yelling foot-stomping and clapping.

3. Jesse really is good at hunting snowmobiling and helping people who get stuck in the snow.

4. Austin Trace and Zack did their homework went to football practice ate dinner at Bud's and watched television until midnight.

5. My favorite pastimes are reading good books golfing in nice weather painting people and eating chocolate.

RULE: _____

1. Everyone is looking forward to snow yet no one is really prepared for it.

2. Riding a bicycle is easy but it also requires coordination.

3. Kim and Rhonda like to perform with the Drill Team but the team doesn't perform very often.

4. Ron said he would buy dinner so Jim said he'd go with him to the restaurant.

5. Neal trained for his wrestling match and won but his good friend didn't.

RULE: _____

1. Our football team is awesome however our volleyball team has been undefeated.

2. Several people are in the running for valedictorian in fact five are tied for the award.

3. Sam won several scholarship awards thus he is one of them.

4. Chad has always done well in math classes therefore he could become a computer programmer.

5. Samantha was late for work three times in a row consequently she thinks she'll be fired.

RULE: _____

1. In his hand he held a fishing rod in his thumb he had the hook.

2. A quiet appearance can be deceiving just ask Debby if this is true.

3. Gary had a hard time buying shoes he wore a size 15.

4. In class he looked like any other student he looked like a character out of a Western movie when riding down Second Street on his horse.

5. The junior class is the largest group at SMHS you might even say they have a lot of class.

Punctuation Worksheet 2 – Commas and Conjunctions

Directions: 1. Circle the **conjunctions**. 2. Punctuate correctly. 3. Write the rule. If no rule applies, write NP (No Punctuation).

_____ 1. Rupert Skraggs Wilfred Hogmire Fats Moon and Clarence Simp made my life miserable in the fourth grade.

_____ 2. I was too young to hunt but I learned some valuable lessons from Scraggs.

_____ 3. I was not the hunter for I was the hunted instead.

_____ 4. Rupert Skraggs would sometimes hunt me for weeks at a time so I had a long apprenticeship as the hunted.

_____ 5. I learned to move quickly sneak silently and cover my trail.

_____ 6. Skraggs stayed in the fourth grade while I was in second third and fourth.

_____ 7. By the time he was finally promoted, he had a beard and sideburns.

_____ 8. Sometimes I managed to shake Rupert off my trail but usually he got me.

_____ 9. Skraggs beat up on the other kids too but I was his favorite.

_____ 10. The other kids learned to act as if the beatings were all in good fun and a welcome relief from their otherwise boring lives.

_____ 11. I never really liked that idea so Skraggs took a serious dislike to me.

_____ 12. Bruce Sid and I decided to challenge him to a fair fight.

_____ 13. Bruce and Sid were fine until Skraggs started rolling up his sleeves.

_____ 14. I was distracted by the sound of running footsteps fading into the distance and then another set of footsteps fading into the distance.

_____ 15. I knew it was fight or flight yet I didn't have any wings.

_____ 16. I finally managed to get away from him and decided to plan a murder.

_____ 17. It would be simple but ingenious and the police would be baffled.

_____ 18. By the time I figured it all out, we were in high school and Skraggs had shrunk.

_____ 19. He got smaller I got bigger and he got nicer.

PUNCTUATION

Subordinate Clauses

Subordinate Clause – A subordinate clause begins with a subordinator (See Special Word Groups List) that is followed by a Sentence Pattern (A complete sentence).

Example: After I ate the donut
A subordinate clause cannot stand alone as a sentence. It must be added to another sentence pattern.

Example: After I ate the donut, I saw visions.

5. **SC, SP**. Because he was late, his mother threw a fit.
   SP SC. His mother threw a fit because he was late.

A subordinate clause can be compound. The subordinator is sometimes *understood* in the second clause.

Example: If I can get my homework done and if I get my chores done, I'll go. Note that the conjunction *and* is joining two **SC**'s, so there is **no** comma in front of it!

Example: If I can get my homework done and I get my chores done, I'll go. Note that "*if* is understood in front of … (*if*)I get my chores done, so it's not possible that the conjunction *and* joins a SC and a SP; conjunctions **always** join two items that are **alike**.

DIRECTIONS: Circle the subordinators, punctuate the sentences correctly, and write the rule in the blank. Be sure to include the **period** (.) at the end of the rule; it's part of the punctuation!

1. Because I was starving I made some chocolate chip cookies. _____

2. After I get home from school I am always really hungry. _____

3. I will eat anything if I can get my hands on it. _____

4. Since I'm always hungry and I'm not particular about what I eat Mom calls me The Human Garbage Disposal. _____

5. I am finally happy as I munch away on leftovers from the refrigerator. _____

6. If there isn't much around to eat I make a brown sugar sandwich. _____

7. Cold mashed potatoes aren't my favorite although I have been known to eat them. _____

8. While I'm not picky I really don't like cold gravy. _____

9. Before I eat gravy it has to be warmed up. _____

10. I am finally completely stuffed as I pass out on the couch. _____

ASSIGNMENT: 1. Write eight (8) sentences, each containing a subordinate clause. 2. Circle the subordinators. 3. Underline the whole subordinate clause. 4. Punctuate correctly. 5. Write the rule. Vary the rule that you use and include at least 3 compound SC's.

IMPORTANT NOTE: The words *before, after, since, until* can be either **subordinators** OR **prepositions**. If followed by a whole sentence pattern, they are **subordinators**; if followed by a noun or noun phrase, they are **prepositions**:

Ex: ... before we went to the football game = SC

... before the game = PP

Conjunctions, Sentence Connectors, and Subordinators
Name _____

Directions: 1. Circle the conjunctions, sentence connectors, and subordinators. 2. Punctuate the sentence. 3. Write the rule that applies. (Don't forget the period, or whatever, **after** the rule. 4. If no rule applies, write **NP** (No Punctuation) in the blank.

_____ 1. When I was young I used to beg my mother to get me a dog.

_____ 2. I knew I had Strange but I wanted a real dog.

_____ 3. Strange had once stopped to beg a free meal and decided to stay on.

_____ 4. He lived with us for ten years although it seemed like centuries to Mom.

_____ 5. Strange was known by our family to be rude crude and socially unacceptable.

_____ 6. I recall one Sunday my mother invited the parish priest to dinner our dining room table overlooked the front yard.

_____ 7. Strange passed by the window not once but twice in fact he walked on his front legs but dragged his rear in the grass.

_____ 8. His mouth was split into an ear-to-ear grin of sublime relief he seemed happy and proud of his discovery of a new treatment for embarrassing itch.

_____ 9. Although she was red-faced Mom tried to distract the pastor by asking how he liked our town.

_____ 10. He appeared not to hear her as he gaped out the window at the disgusting sight.

_____ 11. Strange appeared later with the remains of some creature that had died prior to the previous winter he must have saved it for just such a formal occasion.

_____ 12. As he licked his chops in pretense of preparing to consume the loathsome object Mom's look told me to kill the dog.

_____ 13. I stepped to the door fully intending to carry out the order but Strange ran off snickering.

_____ 14. The dinner was only four courses in length therefore it ended before Strange could stage his grand finale.

_____ 15. Mom said later that she didn't know whether Strange was just more disgusting than usual that day or had something against organized religion.

_____ 16. Strange was the only dog I've known who could belch at will it was his idea of high comedy.

_____ 17. If my mother had some friends over for a game of pinochle Strange would slip into the house.

_____ 18. He would slouch over to the ladies then he would emit a loud belch.

_____ 19. I guess he mistook shudders of revulsion for a form of applause because he would sit there grinning and preparing an encore.

_____ 20. As I dragged him out the back door he muttered and snarled at having to leave such an appreciative crowd.

Series, Two SP's, Subordinate Clauses   Name _____

Directions: Circle all conjunctions, sentence connectors, and subordinators. Insert the correct punctuation. Write the rule that applies in the blank. If no punctuation rule applies, write NP.

_____ 1. A kid by the name of Lester was spending the night with me and we were sleeping on an old mattress out in my back yard.

_____ 2. I had complained of an earache the previous night so my grandmother suggested that I wear something around my head to keep the cold night air from my ear.

_____ 3. Although I possessed half a dozen stocking caps a search of the premises unearthed not a single one of them.

_____ 4. After my grandmother said she would find me something of hers to wear she went to her trunk in the attic and fished out one of her old bonnets.

_____ 5. It was made out of bearskin in fact Grandmother claimed to have worn it on hayrides.

_____ 6. A dog had apparently attacked it before it had been stored in the trunk.

_____ 7. The dog had been either frightened or angry when he managed to tear loose several large chunks of hair.

_____ 8. I didn't want Lester to see me wearing such a monstrosity since he might spread rumors about me around the school yard.

_____ 9. I concealed the hairy bonnet inside my shirt until Lester had dozed off.

_____ 10. Though I had entertained him for several hours with true accounts of several unsolved murders in our neighborhood Lester seemed to sleep rather fitfully.

_____ 11. I then whipped out the bonnet put it on knotted the cords under my chin and slid down under the blankets.

_____ 12. I hoped I would be the first to awaken in the morning in order to remove the headpiece before Lester saw it.

_____ 13. Sometime during the night the bearskin bonnet became twisted on my head leaked cold air into my bad ear and shut off my nose and mouth altogether.

_____ 14. I awoke in a panic of suffocation and tore at the knots under my chin.

_____ 15. There was only one thing to do I lunged toward Lester for help with untying the knots.

_____ 16. I glimpsed Lester through one of the ripped seams in the bearskin his eyelids opened tentatively.

_____ 17. Then both his eyes popped open moreover Lester began to levitate.

_____ 18. After Lester departed I groped my way into the house to my parents' room and shook Mom awake.

_____ 19. I wanted her to help me untie the cords of the hair bonnet that's when the second levitation occurred.

_____ 20. It was less spectacular than Lester's but every bit as good as what a professional magician might do on stage.

PUNCTUATION

Relative Clauses and Prepositional Phrases

Relative Clauses: The five *relatives* (relative pronouns) include *who*, **whom**, *whose*, *which*, and *that*. They introduce relative clauses that are found following a noun either in the middle of a sentence pattern or at the end of a sentence pattern:

Example: … who tried to understand the problem
          … that we found in the closet
          … whom we met for dinner
          … whose billfold got lost
          … which may not be a good idea

6. S *RC* P. and SP*RC. Set a **RC** off with a comma or commas if it is *not needed* to identify the noun in front of it.

Example: The teacher who tried to understand the problem was rewarded.

                This is my new Chevy, *which* I just bought.

                Usually, if the RC is set off with a comma or commas, the *noun* in front of it is **capitalized!**

Usage Note: If a relative clause follows a noun which refers to a **person**, write *who* or *whom* to refer to the person, **not** *that*!

PRACTICE   RELATIVE CLAUSES   NAME_____

DIRECTIONS: Underline the relative clause in each sentence. Put in commas where necessary.

1. That girl is Susie who is an A student.

2. The horse that you see in the stall won the race.

3. The boy who sits in the corner seat is cute.

4. Se climbed into his Jeep which was a total wreck.

5. He is the man who invented the first safety pin.

6. Joe's dog is a pointer which is a hunting breed.

Fix this sentence: People that chew gum with their mouths open are rude crude and unattractive.

7. PP, SP. A prepositional phrase is set off with a comma if it is at the *beginning* of a sentence.

Example: At ten o'clock in the morning, I am usually hungry.

ASSIGNMENT: Write six (6) sentences that begin with prepositional phrases.

PUNCTUATION

Punctuation Rules for Clusters

8: VC, SP. SP, VC. Rule -- **VC** stands for *verb cluster*, a group of words introduced by a verb form, such as "uniting, stuck, blasted." *Verb cluster* is actually just another term for *participial phrase*. Verb clusters usually come at the beginning or end of the sentence. Rule -- **Always** set off VC's with a comma!

Ex: Blasted by Fred's loud rock music, Bertha backhanded Fred. **VC, SP**.

Fred slammed the door, terrified that Bertha would break it down. **SP, VC**.

Note: A *verb cluster* could come in the middle of a sentence pattern, in which case use the rule **S, VC, P**. Ex: Fred, terrified that Bertha would break his head, slammed the door.

9: AC, SP. SP, AC. **AC** stands for *adjective cluster*, a group of words that begins with a true *adjective*, one that has three forms, like "ugly, uglier, ugliest; comfortable, more comfortable, most comfortable." Rule -- <u>Always</u> set off **AC's** with a comma!

Ex: Faster than a speeding turtle, Fred tried to outrun Bertha.
AC, SP.

Bertha was quicker, agile as a cat. **SP, AC**.

10: S, NC, P. SP, NC. Rule -- **NC** stands for *noun cluster*, otherwise known as an *appositive*. The *noun cluster* may start with *a, an*, or *the*, or just **be** a noun.

Rule – **Always** set off *noun clusters* with a comma.

Ex: There sat Brunhilda, Bertha's mother.

Bruce, a friend of Bertha's, was a sumo wrestler.

NOTES: In punctuation Rules 5 through 10, the sentence structure consists of a sentence (SP) to which a group of words has been added. These groups of words are collectively called "Sentence Modifiers."

They include Subordinate Clauses, Relative Clauses, Prepositional Phrases, Verb Clusters, Adjective Clusters, and Noun Clusters.

IMPORTANT: **ANY** sentence that is written or can be written can be punctuated by one of the 10 punctuation rules OR a combination of the rules!!

> Ex: Bertha, who is no small woman, has a terrible temper, terrorizing Fred at every opportunity. S,*RC* P, VC.
>
> OR, more Falkner-esque: Bertha, an individual who is often in error but never in doubt, can be counted on to speak her mind at the drop of a hat, turning the volume up to deafening decibels when she is particularly exercised and emphasizing her rhetoric with much flailing of appendages. S, NC, P, VC SC.

When working with combinations, it is helpful to agree on the convention that writing the combination rule includes **only** those rules that actually prescribe punctuation. In other words, just leave off the SC part above. It is less cumbersome. S, NC, P, VC.

Helpful Hint: When punctuating sentences, first find the SP (or SP's); then look at what's left. You can usually tell from the first word what kind of clause or cluster it is!

> Ex: Fred runs as fast as he can when he sees Bertha.
>
> "Fred runs as fast as he can" is a complete sentence (SP).
>
> "…. when he sees Bertha" is not a sentence. Since it begins with a subordinator (when), it's a Subordinate Clause. The rule is SP SC.

Handy Rules List:

1. Series ___, ___, c ___   6. S* RC* P. SP*RC
2. SP, c SP.   7. PP, SP.
3. SP; sc SP.   8. VC, SP. SP, VC.
4. SP; SP.   9. AC, SP. SP, AC.
5. SC, SP. SP SC.   10. S, NC, P. SP, NC.

Imprint these rules on your brain cells for all eternity!

Punctuating Clusters Assignment   Name_____

1. Write three (3) sentences containing Verb Clusters, underline the clusters, punctuate correctly, and write the rule.

   a. _____

   b. _____

   c. _____

2. Write three sentences containing Adjective Clusters, underline the clusters, punctuate correctly, and write the rule.

   a. _____

   b. _____

   c. _____

3. Write three sentences containing Noun Clusters, underline the clusters, punctuate correctly, and write the rule.

   a. _____

   b. _____

   c. _____

Punctuating Clusters Practice   Name _____

Directions: Find and underline the Sentence Pattern. Identify the kind of Cluster that's left over. (You can call this **chunking** the sentence. Put in correct punctuation, and write the rule at the end in the blank.

Ex: <u>The students began the assignment</u>, wishing they were watching tv and eating pizza. <u>SP, VC.</u>

Write NP in the blank if no punctuation is needed.

1. Driving up in an ancient truck Ketchum Smith watched the smoke puff from every orifice in his rickety vehicle. _____

2. Tough and sinewy Ketchum was as tall a man as I've ever seen. _____.

3. He had a week's worth of gray beard and coal-black eyes glinting out of cavernous sockets. _____.

4. Ketchum did what his name said catching anyone who did him wrong. _____.

5. Ketchum had a meanness to him a serious no-nonsense meanness. _____.

6. Hitchhiking back into the mountains with some loggers to do some fishing Retch and I were to see Ketchum again. _____.

7. We found a pretty little valley with a good stream a perfect place to fish. _____.

8. The loggers seemed unwilling to let us off there uncomfortable about something. _____.

9. We caught lots of beautiful cutthroat hooking them easily. _____.

10. It seemed as though no one had ever fished there before a fisherman's dream. _____.

11. We explored the little valley finding a little cabin someone had built. _____.

12. We decided to investigate scrambling up the slope to the shed. _____.

13. Then we heard someone holler, "Whoa there!" _____.

14. There stood Ketchum Scritch asking us what the tarnation we were doing! _____.

15. Offering to skin us alive if we ever came on his property again Ketchum snatched Retch up by his shirt. _____.

16. Retch's legs were running furiously in mid-air while mine were shaking uncontrollably. _____.

17. Ketchum's made a number of predictions about what he would do to us threats we had no trouble believing. _____.

18. We were so scared that it was a week before we even thought about going back to fish Scritch's creek _____

TRICKSY ELLIPSES

Tricksy Ellipses: Sometimes in a sentence words are omitted that are **understood** to be there in the context of the sentence. This grammar phenomenon can cause confusion.

Throw the cat out. Here, the omission is (you), the "understood" subject; therefore, the group of words is indeed a complete sentence.

If possible, please be here at 9:00. "If (it is) possible," shows the group of words is a Subordinate Clause to be followed by a comma.

After you get home and finish your homework, I will meet you at the river. "After you get home and (after you) finish your homework,..." The conjunction actually joins two Subordinate Clauses.

When he saw Bertha and he realized he couldn't escape, ... "When he saw Bertha and (when) he realized he couldn't escape, ... Same deal.

Mom fixed dinner early so we could all get to the meeting. "... so (that) we could all get to the meeting." <u>So</u> is a conjunction, but <u>so that</u> is a subordinator. No comma in front. Mom fixed dinner at 5:00, so we ate early. <u>So</u> is a conjunction here, and it is preceded by a comma.

She is shorter than I. She is shorter than I (am.) You wouldn't say -- or write -- She is shorter than me (am)!

"Chunking" is helpful when figuring out correct punctuation.

First, find the Sentence Pattern or Patterns:

(Phooter Muldoon wanted to go grouse hunting), but (it was raining). SP, c SP.

Then, look for clauses, clusters, and/or phrases that are left over: (Since the grouse would probably be trying to stay dry), (it would probably be a waste of time). SC, SP. (Phooter, (who was not known for his patience), was totally disgusted.) S* RC* P.

Review 10 Punctuation Rules   Name _____

Directions: Underline conjunctions, sentence connectors and subordinators ONLY!
Put in the correct punctuation.
Write the rule in the blank. Do NOT include **unpunctuated** SC's or RC's in the rules.
Write NP if no punctuation is needed.

1. When Eddie's parents confined him to his own yard for two weeks Crazy Eddie Muldoon and I hit a dead spot in an otherwise interesting summer. _____.

2. This was after Eddie's father had fallen into a pit that we had dug for trapping wild animals intending to tame and train them. _____.

3. Eddie had found an old chair and made a whip out of a stick and a length of clothesline. _____.

4. You needed those things to train wild animals a whip and a chair. _____

5. The idea was to charge people to see the animals perform but then Eddie's father fell into the pit and ruined everything. _____.

6. Mr. Muldoon wasn't even hurt one bit and the skunk wasn't hurt either. _____.

7. The skunk was the only wild animal in the trap at the time not counting Mr. Muldoon. _____.

8. From all the fuss a person would have thought that we had dug the trap just for Eddie's father. _____.

9. It was the trap that got Eddie confined to his yard but I was allowed in to play with him after the first week. _____.

10. Funny as it may seem Eddie was about to go yard crazy. _____.

11. Mr. Muldoon who still could be scented from 50 yards away was still not very happy with us. _____.

12. Mrs. Muldoon explained that we just let our imaginations run away with us sometimes she said we were basically good boys. _____.

13. Mr. Muldoon listened to her however he did not seem convinced. _____.

14. He said that we needed to learn to live life in the real world and not to complain. _____.

15. He said that he never complained. _____.

16. When Eddie's mom asked him to take us to pick huckleberries for jam Eddie's dad started to complain _____.

17. Excited by the prospect of a trip into the big woods Eddie and I ran to get the berry buckets out of the garage. _____.

18. Mr. Muldoon complained even more fiercely it was hard to believe that it was his first time. _____.

19. When Mrs. Muldoon told him to keep an eye on us because it would be easy for us to get lost he chortled evilly. _____.

Punctuation Review

Directions: <u>Underline</u> all conjunctions, sentence connectors, subordinators, relatives, and prepositions (at beginning of sentences). Punctuate according to the rules and write the rule in the blank.

If no punctuation is needed, write NP in the blank.

1. When I saw Phooter Fortner and Ollie Hopnoggin standing next to each other on the risers I knew it wasn't a good thing. _____

2. It was the annual Christmas concert at Delwyn P. Drivel Elementary School. _____

3. As the curtain rose Phooter and Ollie were grinning self-consciously at the audience and elbowing each other in the ribs. _____

4. I noticed frowns on the faces of both Mrs. Fortner and Mrs. Hopnoggin and knew they sensed the impending danger. _____

5. Phooter and Ollie managed to get through the first few numbers without excessive mirth causing Mrs. F and Mrs. H to lower their guards a bit. _____

6. At that point things started to go downhill. _____

7. Mr. Mundy the harried director signaled the children to reach down and put on their Santa hats for the next number. _____

8. Somehow, Phooter and Ollie came up at the same time and cracked heads sending them into gales of giggles. _____

9. Ollie was rubbing his forehead when Phooter pulled his too-large hat down over his eyes. _____

10. He lost his balance grabbing for Ollie and knocking half of the unstable row of third-graders backward. _____

11. Phooter and Ollie received furious looks from their mothers in fact Mrs. Fortner tried unsuccessfully to wade through the audience in an attempt to murder her son. _____

12. The next performance involved Student-of-the-Month Mimi Stinkmouse who read "The Night Before Christmas" next to the Christmas tree. _____

13. Nervous and white-faced she made it to the last line before fainting and toppling the tree as she crumpled to the floor. _____

14. As a couple of frantic teachers dragged Mimi and the tree offstage a commotion was heard in the back of the room. _____

15. It was the grand finale! Santa played by Humpy Hogroll was being pulled in his cardboard sleigh by eight sixth-graders in reindeer costumes. _____

16. They nearly made it to the front of the stage before the sleigh fell apart the result of Humpy's weight and the strain from the reindeers' efforts. _____

17. At that point a perspiring Mr. Mundy implored the audience to join in a rousing rendition of "We Wish You a Merry Christmas." _____

18. It was the best Christmas concert ever! _____

Note: You may need to write a combination rule to punctuate a couple of these!

Punctuation Review Quiz   Name_____

Directions: Underline conjunctions, sentence connectors, and subordinators ONLY!
Put in correct punctuation.
Write the rule in the blank. (Use only the rules for putting in the punctuation. For example, if there are <u>un</u>punctuated SC's or RC's, don't write those rules.)

> Ex: The loving and kind lady who is our teacher told us all to get A's on this test, or she would snatch us bald-headed. <u>SP,c Sp.</u>
> If no punctuation is needed, write NP.

1. You show me a man who fishes in the winter and I'll show you a fanatic. _____.

2. Rancid Crabtree an old mountain man believed in teaching kids the basics of winter fishing. _____.

3. "What you do is stick one foot way out in front of you like this stomping the ice real hard and listening for it to make a cracking sound. _____.

4. "Now pull me up out of here and we'll run back to shore and see if we can build a 'fahr' before I freeze to death!" _____

5. Our usual practice was simply to hike out on the frozen surface of the lake chop a hole in the ice and try to catch some fish. _____.

6. One year we built ourselves a luxurious fishing shack of scrap lumber rusty tin tarpaper and other equally attractive materials. _____.

7. We put a little airtight heater inside because we needed a "fahr." ____.

8. I always expected the stovepipe to set fire to the roof I was not often disappointed. _____.

9. Rancid grubby and scruffy lived alone. _____.

10. Mr. Crabtree had a certain air about him a peculiar aroma.
    _____.

11. Full of colorful expressions Rancid enlarged my vocabulary.
    _____.

12. Crazy as he was he knew a lot about life. _____.

13. Explaining carefully he taught me how to build a "fahr."
    _____.

14. He also showed me how to spot what he called "a iggle" a spectacular bird. _____.

15. Every kid should have his own Rancid Crabtree an old man with time for a kid. _____.

COMBINATION RULES

One of the best things about the 10 punctuation rules is that they can be used individually or in **combination** to punctuate any sentence that can possibly be written!

For example: When I got up, I ate my breakfast, chocolate espresso biscotti with walnuts.

This sentence is made up of a Subordinate Clause, a Sentence Pattern, and a Noun Cluster. Applying the rules … SC, SP, NC. VOILA! Very simple, very easy!

Another example: I am charged with energy as I tackle my morning chores, and I eagerly await "second breakfast" which consists of another chocolate biscotti or two. This sentence includes a Sentence Pattern followed by a Subordinate Clause, a conjunction, and another Sentence Pattern followed by a Relative Clause. Since neither the Subordinate Clause following the first SP is punctuated nor the Relative Clause following the second SP, for simplicity's sake, the rule is written SP, c Sp.

In other words, unpunctuated SC's and RC's are excluded from the formula rule.

This is Grammar for Writing: Since the mechanics of writing as well as matters of style are couched in grammatical terms, writing cannot be taught–or learned–without that knowledge.

Combination Rules Quiz   Name_____

DIRECTIONS: 1. Circle all conjunctions, relatives, and sentence connectors.

2. Circle subordinators and prepositions ONLY when they begin a sentence.

3. Put in the correct punctuation, writing the formula rule in the blank.

4. Remember to <u>exclude</u> unpunctuated relative clauses, subordinate clauses, and prepositional phrases from the formula rule.

1. Ionides a big game hunter also known as Iodine was one of the few who used "solid" non-expanding bullets for lions claiming that they were excellent. _____

2. When he had to kill a man-eater under somewhat unusual circumstances he made this decision and he never regretted it.
_____

3. A fine trophy-quality male had killed a seventeen-year-old girl near a hut and Iodine had been called upon to take care of the situation.
_____

4. This was a well-known man-eater but for reasons known only to him Ionides had sent one of his best scouts to handle things.
_____

5. Waiting for the man-eater to return the scout settled down in the hut getting a shiver each time he looked at the corpse._____

6. It was quite late when the hut shook under the heavy blow of a lion hitting it and trying to get in to take him as well as his prey._____

7. When the hut collapsed burying him under roofing and poles with the lion he was nearly hooked by the big paw._____

8. Luckily, the cat was unable to reach him but the scout spent the remainder of the night beneath hundreds of pounds of poles thatch and heavy mud that was used to hold the hut together._____

9. The lion finally escaped from the hut and the scout followed it up the next morning horribly tense and unnerved._____

10. He managed to wound it sticking a soft point into it as it disappeared from near where the game scout had been waiting for it. _____

11. Ionides had joined the hunt and was tiptoeing on the spoor suddenly the bushes parted and the male came rocketing at him a blur of teeth and mane. _____

12. Ionides was using a .470 Nitro Express and the first shot a soft-point at a close range was later found to glance off the cheek bone and to proceed into the chest where it did no obvious harm._____

13. As a matter of fact the man-eater continued his charge showing no sign of having been hit. _____

14. The lion dodged at a sapling later measured as being eight yards from Ionides and swung around it falling on his nose apparently from the first shot. _____

15. In an instant he was on his feet again and coming as Iodine fired his second and last shot. _____

16. This one hit squarely and the lion was only a couple of paces from the hunter's feet never again did he use soft points for lions._____

Honors English Retest #1 – Combination Punctuation Rules

Name_____

DIRECTIONS: Circle all conjunctions, relatives, and sentence connectors. Also circle prepositions and subordinators IF they begin the sentence. Put in the correct punctuation, and write the rule or combination rule, EXCLUDING unpunctuated RC's, SC's, and PP's.

1. The title for leopard fighting in the heavyweight class unquestionably goes to an American hunter who was named Cottar an ancestor of my friend who operates in Kenya today as a professional._____

2. A huge Oklahoman "Bwana" Cottar as he was called came to Kenya early in this century to be a white hunter and on one occasion choked two leopards to death at the same time one in each hand.
   _____

3. The story goes that one of the leopards had been chewed up in a tussle with the other when Cottar happened along and they decided to take out their differences on the Bwana._____

4. Considering that the Oklahoman liked to do his leopard wrestling after a few belts his success is even more fantastic._____

5. Cottar was a man who took his hunting seriously. _____

6. Around dusk one night he wounded a leopard on his farm and followed it into the bush._____

7. As one might expect he got the blazes bitten out of him and the cat ran off into the gathering darkness._____

8. Wrapping the tatters of his shirt around his wounds Cottar repaired to the farmhouse and broke out a bottle of 100-proof cure all._____

9. In a couple of hours he had drunk most of it and fuming over the failure of having lost the cat he cracked open another quart._____

10. About halfway through this one he finally decided to heck with it picked up his rifle and kerosene lantern and went crashing out into the stormy night._____

11. Stamping around the thick bush and commenting on the ancestry of the cat he found it or it found him._____

12. It showed no hesitancy in trying to shred Cottar again but this time he managed to shove the muzzle against its chest and finish it off.
_____

13. After a couple of years the Bwana had another meeting with a cat that cost him the use of his right arm through terrible injuries by the leopard. _____

14. Undaunted to the end Cottar learned to shoot with his left until gored in the heart by a rhino in later life._____

(...adapted from <u>Death in the Long Grass</u> by Peter Hathaway Capstick)

Honors English Final: Combination Punctuation Rules Name_____

Directions: Circle all conjunctions, relatives, and sentence connectors. Also circle subordinators IF they begin the sentence. Put in the correct punctuation, and write the rule or combination rule, EXCLUDING unpunctuated RC's, SC's, and PP's.

1. The title for leopard fighting in the heavyweight class unquestionably goes to an American hunter who was named Cottar an ancestor of my friend who operates in Kenya today as a professional. _____

2. A huge Oklahoman "Bwana" Cottar as he was called came to Kenya early in this century to be a white hunter and on one occasion choked two leopards to death at the same time one in each hand.
   _____

3. The story goes that one of the leopards had been chewed up in a tussle with the other when Cottar happened along and they decided to take out their differences on the Bwana._____

4. Considering that the Oklahoman liked to do his leopard wrestling after a few belts his success is even more fantastic._____

5. Cottar was a man who took his hunting seriously._____

6. Around dusk one night he wounded a leopard on his farm and followed it into the bush._____

7. As one might expect he got the blazes bitten out of him and the cat ran off into the gathering darkness._____

8. Wrapping the tatters of his shirt around his wounds Cottar repaired to the farmhouse and broke out a bottle of 100-proof cure-all.
   _____

9. In a couple of hours he had drunk most of it and fuming over the failure of having lost the cat he cracked open another quart.
   _____

10. About halfway through this one he finally decided to heck with it picked up his rifle and kerosene lantern and went crashing out into the stormy night. _____

11. Stamping around the thick bush and commenting on the ancestry of the cat he found it or it found him. _____

12. It showed no hesitancy in trying to shred Cottar again but this time he managed to shove the muzzle against its chest and finish it off.
_____

13. After a couple of years the Bwana had another meeting with a cat that cost him the use of his right arm a result of terrible injuries by the leopard. _____

14. Undaunted to the end, Cottar leaned to shoot with his left until gored in the heart by a rhino in later life. _____

(... adapted from <u>Death in the Long Grass</u> by Peter Hathaway Capstick)